His Spirit in You
Eight Personalities in Acts

His Spirit in You

Eight Personalities in Acts

by

Merrill S. Williams

Beacon Hill Press of Kansas City
Kansas City, Missouri

Copyright 1982
by Beacon Hill Press of Kansas City

ISBN: 0-8341-0783-X

Printed in the United States of America

Cover design by: Royce Ratcliff

Permission to quote from the following copyrighted versions of the Bible is acknowledged with appreciation:

The Holy Bible, New International Version (NIV), copyright © 1978 by New York International Bible Society.

The *New American Standard Bible* (NASB), © The Lockman Foundation, 1960, 1962, 1968, 1971, 1972, 1973, 1975, 1977.

Unless otherwise noted, all Scripture quotations in this text are from the *New International Version.*

DEDICATION

To Jan
 Who exemplifies the Spirit-filled life
  and warms my heart and our home
  with her love

Contents

1. Conspiracy of Deception	9
2. Stephen, We Never Knew You	17
3. The Spirit Has the Lead	24
4. Conquered by Love	32
5. What Happened on the Street Called Straight?	38
6. The Sermon That Was Interrupted	45
7. Footprints of the Spirit	51
8. A Preacher Gets Filled with the Spirit	60
Reference Notes	67

Ananias and Sapphira
Acts 4:32—5:11

1

Conspiracy of Deception

One ugly blemish blots the smooth complexion of the Spirit-filled Early Church. Jesus' disciples were taking such leaping strides that when this event disrupted their advance, it shook the young Church to its very foundations.

And, although we cannot dismiss this unfortunate incident, we can learn a valuable lesson from it. This tragic event illustrates that the Church consists of real people who live in a real world. It is not a spiritual utopia, a glass tower where ill winds never blow.

A court painter was commissioned to paint the portrait of the British statesman Oliver Cromwell. Cromwell's face was marked with warts. Thinking to please his subject, the artist omitted the facial flaws. When Cromwell saw the picture, he said, "Take it away and paint me warts and all."[1] The biblical writers deserve credit for painting the portraits of their heroes and heroines "warts and all."

The Community of Disciples

In Acts 5:11 Luke will first use the word "church" in his account to identify Jesus' disciples. In 4:32-37, however, he embodies the basic principle of the church—a community of disciples. What characterizes the community of disciples, then and now?

Unity characterizes this community. "All the believers were one in heart and mind" (v. 32). What more appropriate place for people to exhibit a unanimous spirit than the church? Where else do men expect such a marriage of human hearts? Have not Christians surrendered themselves to Christ? Have they not subordinated their wills to His? Have they not dedicated themselves to spiritual oneness?

Such a posture does not mean disagreements will never occur. Even sanctified, Spirit-filled individuals sometimes disagree over methods. But motives should never conflict. Among the truly sanctified, intentions are pure, cleansed by the Holy Spirit.

Generosity also characterizes this community. "No one claimed that any of his possessions was his own, but they shared everything they had" (ibid.). Their spiritual unity produced a social community. This in no way implies that the Early Church practiced a form of communism. No one forced them to sell their possessions and pool them for the public good; divine love motivated them to give, voluntarily, to others in need.

These early disciples didn't practice communism, they practiced responsible Christian stewardship. If a need arose, a disciple made money available to meet that need. W. Graham Scroggie writes, "Never, when the heart has been open, has the pocket been closed."[2]

While the method of distribution has changed, the principle remains—generosity to those in need. Apparently "those who owned lands or houses sold them, brought the money from the sales and put it at the apostles' feet, and it was distributed to anyone as he had need" (Acts 4:34-35). The first Christians would literally "rather have Jesus than houses or lands"!

In addition, *bravery* characterizes the community of disciples. "With great power the apostles continued to testify to the resurrection of the Lord Jesus" (v. 33). God answered their sincere prayer of v. 29: "Now, Lord, consider their threats and enable your servants to speak your word with great boldness." They didn't pray for protection but for power, power to proclaim the risen Christ. A new life throbbed in their hearts, and they wanted desperately to share it.

When the Holy Spirit comes in His fullness, we may expect Him to come with power. He will not only cleanse our hearts from all sin; He will also empower us to share His love with others. The last words our Lord spoke before He ascended back to the Father were these: "But you will receive power, when the Holy Spirit comes on you; and you will be my witnesses" (1:8). This prayer ought to rise spontaneously from the heart of every Christian, "Lord, empower me this day to witness effectively for You."

Sanctity also characterizes the church. "And great grace was upon them all" (4:33, KJV). What a spiritual epitaph! If a thousand years from now the world could say the same of us, we should be more than pleased. The testimony of their lips complemented the testimony of their lives. The faithful disciple today backs up his testimony with his life.

The Conspiracy of Deceit

Luke slows and diverts the flow of thought with the contrastive word "But" (5:1, KJV, NASB). Barnabas and

Ananias provide a study in contrasts. Luke deliberately intends to set these two men in opposition—Barnabas commended, Ananias condemned.

Who are the characters in this drama of deceit? A husband-wife team named Ananias and Sapphira. They were, no doubt, respectable members in their local church. Their names, however, reveal nothing of their true character.

Ananias means "God is gracious." Yet this one, to whom God gave grace, terribly disappointed his Benefactor. Sapphira means "beautiful." Yet she was so much unlike the beautiful gem after which she was named. Whatever beauty she possessed—whether physical or spiritual—soon shattered in the cold chill of hypocrisy.

What was their script? How would they play out their parts? Seeing a need in the church, Barnabas sold a piece of property and brought the proceeds to the apostles to distribute as needed. Ananias and Sapphira, seeing the approval Barnabas received from their peers, also sold a piece of property. So far, so good; nothing wrong yet.

But instead of bringing the entire purchase price to the apostles, they brought only part of it. They kept the rest for themselves. As Peter will declare, they still had not done anything wrong. It was their land. They could do with it as they pleased. The money they received for its sale belonged to them. They were not required to give a part, if any, to the church.

Their sin was not in giving part of the price, but in giving only part and *saying they had given all*. The word translated here "kept back" is the same word used in the Greek translation of the Old Testament of Achan who "took of the accursed thing" (Josh. 7:1, KJV) from the city of Jericho. He appropriated something for personal use that was devoted to God.

Ananias and Sapphira deliberately lied to the Holy

Spirit. Peter's question reveals their deplorable act: "How is it that Satan has so filled your heart that you have lied to the Holy Spirit . . . ?" (Acts 5:3). The Holy Spirit is not just an impersonal power, or a faraway influence, but a Person. A thing cannot be lied to; a person can. Peter says that when they tried to deceive the Church, they had "not lied to men but to God" (v. 4).

Peter rightly asks a subsequent question, and we join him in his query. Why? Why would a person lie to the Holy Spirit and seek to deceive Him?

They were dishonest with the Holy Spirit because Satan had filled their hearts with a lie. Just as Satan entered into Judas to move him to the world's most abhorrent duplicity (Luke 22:3), so the father of lies (John 8:44) filled the hearts of Ananias and Sapphira with a lie. What tragic irony there is here. Luke employs the same word for "fill" here as he does in Acts 4:31 for the filling of the Holy Spirit! These who could have been filled with the Holy Spirit were filled instead with a devilish lie—that a person can deceive the Holy Spirit and get away with it. If they could only have seen the futility of their attempt.

Jesus said someone will indwell the human spirit, and Satan will fill any person who will not be filled with the Holy Spirit. Martin Luther said rather indelicately, "Man is a saddle-horse. Either God or the devil will ride him." Unless the vacuum of the human spirit is filled with the Holy Spirit, "the final condition of that man is worse than the first" (Matt. 12:45).

Another motivating factor in their conspiracy was greed. Ananias and Sapphira loved their money, and Paul said that the *love* of money is the root of all evil. Certainly its roots grew into a horrible species of greed in the lives of Ananias and Sapphira.

Greed's thirst is never quenched. Leo Tolstoy tells the story of a man who was told he could have all the land he could cover on foot in a day's time. He started out walking. But as his desire for additional land consumed him, he began to run. At day's end, he had covered many acres—only to drop dead from exhaustion!

The desire for material gain runs a malevolent cycle. The more a person gets, the more he wants; the more he wants, the more he seeks to get. Unending, enslaving, damning.

Pride also motivated their deceit. Like many modern-day Christians they labored under the burden to "keep up with the Barnabases." They saw how the church applauded Barnabas, and they too wanted some of the glory. A. T. Robertson writes of Ananias, "He wanted praise for giving all and yet he took care of himself by keeping some."[3]

Ananias types—those who want to be identified with the fully committed but who do not want to actually give all—are still with us. They recognize and appreciate the glory bestowed by the church upon the one who makes a full surrender to God. But the price is too high. They may feign wholehearted commitment. They may even make a public display of their supposed surrender. But give all? No, not quite. "Just let me reserve . . . ," they say.

In the end, however, the deceit of Ananias and Sapphira was self-motivated. Both Luke and Peter accuse Ananias of keeping part of the purchase price for "himself." Although Satan tempted the pair, they must assume the full and final responsibility for their act. Either the couple had not allowed the Holy Spirit to cleanse their hearts and fill their lives, or they had withdrawn some of their commitment, and He had withdrawn from them. The Holy Spirit is slow to leave the hospitable heart. But when He is deliberately deceived, He has no other choice; His character demands it.

The Consequences of Disobedience

What happened to Ananias and Sapphira as a result of their deception has long puzzled Bible students. While it is undeniably true that "the wages of sin is death" (Rom. 6:23), and that "whatsoever a man soweth, that shall he also reap" (Gal. 6:7, KJV), what happened to these two defies dogmatic explanation.

What killed Ananias and Sapphira? It could easily be that God struck them instantly dead. He probably did. And while I have no desire to bleed this incident of its miraculous element, I mention another possibility.

In an article published in *Reader's Digest* entitled, "Can Your Emotions Kill You?" Dr. George Engel writes, "As far back as written records exist, people are described as dying suddenly while in the throes of fear, rage, grief, humiliation, or joy."[4]

Dr. Engel compiled 275 cases of death immediately following major events in people's lives. Most of the victims were not ill, or if they were, they were certainly not in danger of dying. Four categories emerged into which each of the cases fit. The third category—which accounted for 21 of the cases—was "sudden death in the wake of disappointment, failure, defeat, loss of status or self-esteem."[5]

E. Stanley Jones believed that the spiritual atmosphere in the Church at this time was so charged that when Ananias and Sapphira defied it, they died of heart failure—not by a stroke from God, but from a stroke from within!

In addition to her own guilt for her part in the plot, Sapphira was forced to face the sudden announcement her husband had died only hours before. Dr. Engel classified deaths in the first category—the majority of them, 135—in terms of the disruption of a close personal relationship. Fifty-seven of those 135 died *immediately after the collapse or death of a loved one!*

It is, therefore, in the realm of possibility that the disobedience of Ananias and Sapphira caused such psychosomatic trauma that they died as a result. But whether they died by the direct intervention of God or from heart failure, their example illustrates our personal responsibility to God, especially to God the Holy Spirit.

We have an awesome responsibility to live under the Spirit's control and be absolutely honest with Him at all times. Paul's admonition speaks clearly in any age: "Do not grieve the Holy Spirit of God" (Eph. 4:30).

The tragedy of Ananias and Sapphira was not that they died suddenly and violently, but that they were dishonest with the Spirit of truth (John 16:13). If only they had surrendered to Him and allowed Him to guide them into all truth, they would have lived. But because of their deceit, they not only lost physical life, they also forfeited eternal life. In our relationship with the Holy Spirit, honesty is, indeed, the best policy.

2

Stephen
Acts 6:8-15; 7:54-60

Stephen, We Never Knew You

One of the greatest tragedies of life is the premature death of a person who bears the marks of greatness. We wonder of such a person: "How much more could he have accomplished if life had not left him so soon?" Who knows what seed of potential lay dormant in the bosom of young Stephen?

To undiscerning eyes he died before he accomplished the great purposes for which he was destined. But to the One who sees beyond the frail curtain of humanity, Stephen's life was not lost. He did accomplish God's purpose. Maybe he would never have touched the world as he did if he had not died when he did. He spoke the truth who said, "Stephen's prayer gave Paul to the Church."

Stephen, we never knew you—or did we? Let's follow the course of this Spirit-filled layman's life and see if he doesn't lead us to heights of spiritual character.

Selected for Service

Stephen was selected for service *because the Church had a need*. Still, a sure sign of a divine call to Christian service—whether full-time or as a dedicated layman—is a recognition of human need.

The Church had swelled in membership, and some of the problems that accompany growth had arisen. The Greek-speaking Christians began to complain because they felt the Church favored the Aramaic-speaking widows in the daily food dole and neglected their widows.

The apostles, therefore, called the Church together and made this suggestion: Appoint seven men, full of the Holy Spirit and wisdom, to oversee this operation, and leave us free for prayer and the study of the Word. Pleased with this proposal, the Church selected Stephen, Philip, and five others. They must have chosen wisely, because after that the Word was proclaimed to more people, new disciples were produced, and even their opposition was persuaded to join them! (Acts 6:7).

Stephen was also selected for service *because God had a man*. Stephen stepped into that long line of men and women who have made themselves available for God's service.

What qualified Stephen for spiritual service?

He possessed wisdom (Acts 6:3), faith (v. 5), grace (v. 8), and power (ibid.). All these qualities of character made Stephen eligible for effective service. But God's power, working in and through him, enabled him to do "great wonders and miraculous signs among the people" (ibid.). Jesus promised His disciples abundant power in the Holy Spirit (1:8), and Stephen surely proved that promise true.

Twice Luke describes Stephen as a man filled with the Holy Spirit (6:5; 7:55). The fullness of the Spirit enabled

Stephen to minister to the multitudes and to face triumphantly the angry antagonism of his persecutors. And the same Spirit who filled Stephen's life wants to flow into the life of every Christian disciple to cleanse, comfort, strengthen, and make adequate for life's demands.

Seized by Enemies

But a Grecian Jew preaching Jesus as the Messiah endeared no friends at the Synagogue of the Freedmen. Rather, Stephen aroused their opposition, and they began to argue with him.

First, there was *dissension.* This synagogue comprised former slaves, or their descendants, who had been freed and now worshipped together. Since Cilicians were represented, it may have been that Saul, also from Cilicia, joined in the dispute.

Defeat followed the dissension. Although they marshalled their best arguments, "they could not stand up against his wisdom or the Spirit by which he spoke" (Acts 6:10). As Stephen debated, he must have remembered a saying of the Master, "For I will give you words and wisdom that none of your adversaries will be able to resist or contradict" (Luke 21:15). At the exhilarating thought of Jesus' promise, new strength and power surely surged through Stephen.

Apart from the anointing of God's Spirit, not even the most able and articulate orator can persuade men to surrender their lives to the Lordship of Christ. How much more, then, do we need His power to witness effectively for Him. Spiritual achievement comes "not by might, nor by power, but by my spirit, saith the Lord" (Zech. 4:6, KJV).

Then, there was *deceit.* Since his opponents could not best him honestly, they resorted to treachery. They hired false witnesses to say, "This fellow never stops speaking against the holy place and against the law. For we have heard him say that this Jesus of Nazareth will destroy this place and change the customs Moses handed down to us" (Acts 6:13-14).

These so-called witnesses presented two charges that would have quickly aroused the ire of the people. They claimed Stephen threatened two of their most important national institutions—the Temple and the Law.

Caiaphas, the high priest, produced two false witnesses who brought similar charges against Jesus. They charged that Jesus had claimed, "I am able to destroy the temple of God and rebuild it in three days" (Matt. 26:61). Jesus had actually said, "(You) destroy this temple, and I will raise it again in three days" (John 2:19). Jesus referred not to their Temple, but to His body. Both men, therefore—Jesus and Stephen—were convicted by false witnesses who testified to half truths.

But there was also *dignity*. Stephen stood accused. Every eye turned toward him to see his reaction and hear his response to these serious charges. What they saw surprised, astonished, and intimidated them. "They saw that his face was like the face of an angel" (Acts 6:15). He stood alone, but he was not really alone. Jesus was there!

Stephen's countenance must have resembled Moses' when he returned from Mount Sinai. As he descended, "Moses did not know that the skin of his face shone because of his speaking with Him" (Exod. 34:29, NASB).

If the Holy Spirit does anything for the believer, He fortifies him for the pressures of daily living. He gives serenity in strife, calm in conflict, tranquility in turmoil.

Stoned to Death

When Stephen had finished his defense, the people *raged with fury.* "They were furious and [ground] their teeth at him" (Acts 7:54). The truth sometimes hurts, and Stephen had driven the truth deep into their hearts.

Like wild animals (cf. Luke 8:33) they "rushed at him, dragged him out of the city and began to stone him" (Acts 7:57-58). How unlike these, who rushed at him in unison, were those in Jerusalem at Pentecost who "were all together" (2:1) for the purpose of receiving the gift of the Holy Spirit!

The Jewish punishment for blasphemy was death by stoning (Lev. 24:14-16). Stephen's accusers muscled him outside the city—possibly to the hill of Calvary—to the place of stoning. Stephen would not be stoned by everyone indiscriminately. The law provided that the first witness push the convicted person off a rock as high as two men. If the fall did not kill him, then the witnesses would throw a large stone on him, one they could barely lift together. So the two witnesses cast the first stones upon the first witness (martyr) for Christ.

But while the crowd raged with fury, Stephen *rested in faith.* The contrast was evident: the crowd stirred to a frenzy, and Stephen stable under pressure.

In these circumstances Stephen saw his Savior. "But Stephen . . . looked up to heaven and saw . . . Jesus . . . 'Look,' he said, 'I see heaven open and the Son of Man standing at the right hand of God'" (Acts 7:55-56).

He possibly had never met Jesus personally, but when he saw Him, he recognized Him. We really don't know what Jesus looked like either. But there is no doubt that when we see Him, we shall know Him. Fanny Crosby pictured that meeting:

> *When my lifework is ended, and I cross the swelling tide,*
> *When the bright and glorious morning I shall see,*
> *I shall know my Redeemer when I reach the other side,*
> *And His smile will be the first to welcome me.*

Stephen recognized Jesus as far more than the Jewish Messiah. He knew that Jesus' reign would extend far beyond the provincial borders of Judaism, that He would indeed rule the world. Stephen knew that he witnessed to a Savior who had opened the way directly to God and made obsolete all the sacrificial ritual of the Temple.

All references to Jesus at the Father's side picture Him *seated*, signifying His finished work of salvation for men (Matt. 26:64; Mark 16:19; Acts 2:34; Eph. 1:20; Col. 3:1; Heb. 1:3; 10:12). But Stephen saw Him *standing*. Why?

He stood as a witness for Stephen's defense. Stephen stood condemned and appealing to a higher court, and Jesus stood—the proper posture for a witness—to act as his Paraclete, his Advocate. Against every accusation of Satan Jesus still acts as our Advocate, defending us. John wrote, "We have an Advocate with the Father, Jesus Christ the righteous" (1 John 2:1, NASB).

Jesus also stood to honor Stephen, to welcome him home and give him the crown of life (Rev. 2:10). When we have fought our last battle, when we have resisted our last temptation, when we have beaten our last enemy, Jesus will be waiting to welcome us home.

When Stephen had seen his Savior, he surrendered his life to Him. Long ago he had taken the Way, and here is where it had led him. When he first surrendered his life to Christ, he did not know it would lead him to a martyr's death. He didn't know where it would lead. But he had promised to follow, and his present circumstances didn't deter him. He still served, still trusted, still loved the Master who had saved him.

Is our faith as great? Does our confidence hold so firm? Do we trust Him enough to follow where His Spirit leads? The Holy Spirit strengthens our faith and enables us to commit ourselves wholeheartedly to His will. If they had been written, Stephen would have surely sung the words of Jessie B. Pounds' hymn:

Anywhere with Jesus I can safely go,
Anywhere He leads me in this world below.
Anywhere without Him dearest joys would fade.
Anywhere with Jesus I am not afraid.

Philip
Acts 8:26-40

3

The Spirit Has the Lead

Stephen—dead.

Philip, the Spirit-filled layman, felt the weight of sorrow deep in the pit of his stomach. He would ever after chronicle time by Stephen's death because "on that day a great persecution broke out against the church at Jerusalem" (Acts 8:1).

Of that harassment Alexander Maclaren writes, "Men tried to fling down the lamp; and all that they did was to spill the oil, and it ran flaming wherever it flowed."[1]

Philip's Response to the Enemy's Persecution

A young Jew from Tarsus named Saul led the assault against the Church. "Going from house to house, he dragged off men and women and put them in prison"

(v. 3). So when the first brutal wave of persecution smashed against the fellowship, to avoid his rage, "all except the apostles were scattered throughout Judea and Samaria" (v. 1).

Philip joined those who made their way north from Jerusalem about 30 miles to the city of Samaria. Once there, he began to witness to Christ, his Savior. To confirm his testimony, God gave him the special ability to perform miracles. He freed the demon-possessed from their bondage and healed the sick of their afflictions (vv. 6-7).

When Spirit-filled persons proclaim the gospel, some will exercise faith and be saved. So it was in Samaria. Many believed Philip's message and were converted and baptized (v. 12).

Deep joy also accompanies a genuine faith in Christ. The contagion of Philip's experience in the Holy Spirit spread through the entire city until this important fruit of the Spirit—joy—began to thrive in the hearts of the new converts (v. 8; Gal. 5:22).

Philip's Response to the Spirit's Direction

Although God used an angel to speak to Philip, He required a Spirit-filled, flesh-and-blood man to minister to one whose heart hungered for spiritual reality. We ought not to expect God to answer our prayers without our cooperation. The Acts account clearly illustrates that the Holy Spirit works through human instruments, and we will often be the answers to our own prayers.

Philip is a living example of a person led by the Holy Spirit.

The Spirit led Philip to the right *place*. "Now an angel of the Lord said to Philip, 'Go south to the road—the desert road--that goes down from Jerusalem to Gaza'" (Acts 8:26).

Although, like Abraham, he didn't know where he was going, he started out in obedience to the Holy Spirit. We may not always know our destination when we start to obey the Spirit, but we do know that where God calls us, He will safely carry us.

The Spirit also led Philip to the right *person*. "On his way he met an Ethiopian eunuch" (v. 27). The eunuch served as treasurer for Candace, queen of Ethiopia. He was returning from a pilgrimage to Jerusalem. He was probably a "God-fearer"—one who was sympathetic to the Jewish religion.

Philip had reached his divine rendezvous. "The Spirit told Philip, 'Go to that chariot and stay near it'" (v. 29). Does it seem strange that the Spirit would lead Philip away from a place where *many* were being converted to a place where only *one* would be saved? But Jesus said that one human life is more valuable than the whole world (Matt. 16:26).

A simple tabernacle stands unassuming and unknown on the Fort Jessop Campground outside Many, La. Many years ago a revival was scheduled there. Money was not readily available, however, and someone suggested they could not really afford to pay an evangelist that year. But one woman offered to sell her only cow to finance that revival. When the evangelist had gone, only one young boy had been converted. It hardly seemed worth the expense. But that one boy grew up to be R. T. Williams, general superintendent in the Church of the Nazarene—and he ministered to thousands. The R. T. Williams Tabernacle testifies to the value of one person's worth in the sight of God.

Some say the Ethiopian eunuch started the church in his part of Africa. Others say there is no evidence of the church existing there until the fourth century A.D. No doubt, however, he did share his faith with others in his homeland. But even if he had not, God thought one individual important enough to send Philip toward Gaza to win him to Christ.

Also, the Spirit led Philip to the right *scripture*. "This man had gone to Jerusalem to worship, and on his way home was sitting in his chariot reading the book of Isaiah the prophet" (Acts 8:27-28). In His providence, God had led the Ethiopian to Isaiah's prophecy, chapter 53. It fully expounds the redemptive ministry of Jesus, the Messiah.

A scroll of Isaiah was found in the caves at Qumran near the Dead Sea in 1947. It was intact and dated back to the second century B.C. Since scrolls were so expensive to produce, only a wealthy person like the eunuch could afford to own one.

Philip took this opportunity to approach the chariot and ask the man if he understood what he was reading. The Ethiopian replied, "'Well, how could I, unless someone guides me?'" (v. 31, NASB). This treasurer now held a precious treasure in his hands, but he couldn't unearth its meaning. He could read the words, but he could not decipher their significance. Although open in his lap, the scroll was closed to his unenlightened eyes. He needed a spiritual guide.

But because he wanted to understand, the Holy Spirit sent Philip to aid his search. The word translated "guide" here is the same word Jesus uses to describe the ministry of the Spirit. "But when he, the Spirit of truth, comes, he will *guide* you into all truth" (John 16:13).

Just as Philip guided the Ethiopian toward the truth, so the Holy Spirit—our spiritual Guide—will direct our way. Under His tutelage, the Bible opens and reveals its eternal truth.

So the eunuch asked Philip, "'Tell me, please, who is the prophet talking about, himself or someone else?' Then Philip began with that very passage of Scripture and told him the good news about Jesus" (Acts 8:34-35).

In our efforts to witness for Christ, we need to pray that the Holy Spirit will lead us to the right scripture, the verse or verses that will lift up Christ as Savior. Jesus said, "Do not worry beforehand about what to say. Just say whatever is given you at the time, for it is not you speaking, but the Holy Spirit" (Mark 13:11).

In addition, the Spirit led Philip at the right *time*. If Philip had not left Samaria when the Spirit prompted him, if he had delayed his departure, this account might read differently. If Philip had not arrived at the exact time the Ethiopian was passing on that road, he would have already travelled slowly out of his reach, and might never have found Christ.

Not only did the Spirit lead Philip, He also led the Ethiopian. God the Holy Spirit caused their paths to intersect that day. How often does God intend our path to cross that of one who needs our help? No accident brought Saul and Ananias together in that home in Damascus. Chance had nothing to do with Peter preaching to Cornelius and his household. The Holy Spirit—working at both ends—brought them together. Let us be sensitive to the Spirit's promptings. He may intend us to meet the right person at the right time of spiritual need.

Finally, the Spirit led Philip to the right *conclusion*. "As they travelled along the road, they came to some water and the eunuch said, 'Look, here is water. Why shouldn't I be baptized?' And he ordered the chariot to stop. Then both Philip and the eunuch went down into the water and Philip baptized him" (Acts 8:36-38).

As Philip had expounded the gospel, he had also explained that baptism follows conversion. It symbolizes a cleansing, a clean break with the old life, a new union with Christ (Rom. 6:3-5). The Early Church knew of no unbaptized Christians.

As the Spirit whisked Philip away to Azotus, the Ethiopian didn't appear at all distressed. Most likely—if this event is consistent with the rest of Acts—the eunuch soon received the baptism with the Holy Spirit. He, therefore, had a better Guide, one who would lead him into all truth. And he "went on his way rejoicing" (Acts 8:39).

Compare the joy of salvation with the sorrow of rejection by another man of wealth. The rich young ruler who had come to Jesus seeking eternal life "went away sad" (Matt. 19:22). Haldor Lillenas pleads for all to follow the way that leads to joy:

> *Patiently, tenderly pleading,*
>   *Jesus is standing today;*
> *At your heart's door He knocks as before.*
>   *Oh, turn Him no longer away!*
>
> *Don't turn Him away.*
>   *Don't turn Him away.*
> *He has come back to your heart again,*
>   *Although you've gone astray.*
>
> *Oh, how you'll need Him to plead your cause*
>   *On that eternal day!*
> *Don't turn the Savior away from your heart;*
>   *Don't turn Him away.*

Copyright 1925. Renewed 1953 by Lillenas Publishing Co. All rights reserved.

Philip's Response to the Lord's Commission

After Philip's encounter with the Ethiopian, we do not hear of him again until 20 years later. He made Caesarea his home and raised four daughters who followed their father in a preaching ministry.

A solitary verse in Acts 21 and Philip's noticeable absence in the 20-year interim imply two important things about the continuing ministry of the Holy Spirit in a person's life.

First, the Holy Spirit helps us *apply sanctified common sense* in many situations of life. Many times through those years of spiritual labor, the Spirit must have led Philip not by dramatic, abnormal means, but in ordinary, normal ways.

J. Sidlow Baxter writes:

> After all, the highest and truest form of guidance is not that which comes by intermittent abnormalities, but that which comes *continually* by the electric current of the Holy Spirit flowing through our own consecrated faculties of reason and conscience. When our mental and moral faculties are really consecrated to Christ, *then* the Holy Spirit can guide us best of all through our own natural faculties. . . . The more *naturally* we allow ourselves to be guided by the Holy Spirit, the better. . . . The intendedly normal way of guidance is for the Holy Spirit to guide the consecrated believer through the natural functioning of enlightened perception, reason, judgment, conscience, decision.[2]

Second, the Holy Spirit helps us *accept unnoticed labor.* When Philip had fulfilled his task of winning the Ethiopian eunuch to Christ, the account turns from Philip and focuses more prominently on others, mainly Peter and Paul. How did Philip respond to this obscurity? Did he become bitter and vow not to labor if he could not be more prominent?

Philip was probably present in Caesarea when God's angel spoke to Cornelius (Acts 10:1). Did Philip become disgruntled because Cornelius sent for Peter instead of him? No. The Holy Spirit helped Philip accept a place of lesser prominence in God's evangelistic strategy.

Philip won the first Gentile to Christianity, but Paul became the apostle to the Gentiles. Did Philip pout and sulk and hold a grudge against his co-worker? Apparently not. For, 20 years afterward, when Paul came to Caesarea on one of his missionary trips, Philip welcomed him into his home (Acts 21:8).

The Holy Spirit helped Philip understand that some plant, some water, and others harvest. Paul wrote, "The man who plants and the man who waters have one purpose, and each will be rewarded according to his own labor" (1 Cor. 3:8).

Both when he dominated the center of attention and through the "hidden" years of his life, Philip walked deliberately, persistently, and patiently with the Holy Spirit, and the Holy Spirit walked with him.

Paul
Acts 9:1-9

Conquered by Love

As the sun topped the horizon, Paul (at first known as Saul) and his escort of Roman guards had already been on the road several hours. They had begun early marching toward Damascus, a city 70 miles from the Mediterranean and 200 miles north of Jerusalem.

On this, the sixth day of their journey, they neared their destination, and Paul eagerly anticipated the arrest of more heretical "Christians."

Jacob had predicted, "Benjamin shall ravin as a wolf" (Gen. 49:27, KJV). If confronted, he would have vehemently denied it, but Paul was fulfilling that prophecy. He confidently believed he was doing the will of God. Later he would testify that he persecuted the Church out of loyalty to God (Acts 22:3).

Little did Paul know, however, that he had pursued his last prisoner, stalked his last quarry, murdered his last martyr. He could not have known that Another had been stalking him, and that soon the capturer would be the captured.

Conviction

The New Testament refers little to the Holy Spirit's ministry in the lives of unbelievers. But, in the most comprehensive passage on the subject, Jesus describes the primary activity of the Holy Spirit in relation to the world. "And He, when He comes, will convict the world concerning sin, and righteousness, and judgment" (John 16:8, NASB).

In *God, Man, and Salvation* the authors write of this passage, "The word 'convict . . . ,' in this instance, means 'to convict, confute, refute, usually with the suggestion of putting the convicted person to shame.' It thus is stronger than 'convince' (RSV). . . . Apparently the truth is not enough. The truth must be thrust into the conscience and enforced upon the mind by the Spirit."[1]

The Holy Spirit convicts the unbeliever in different ways. He often employs *the Word of God* to awaken the conscience. Paul later wrote, "My message and my preaching were not with wise and persuasive words, but with a demonstration of the Spirit's power" (1 Cor. 2:4). Peter also attributes life-changing power to the Word energized by the Spirit. He spoke of those "who have preached the gospel to you by the Holy Spirit" (1 Pet. 1:12).

The Spirit jolts many a person out of their unconcern and spiritual apathy by the potent application of God's Word. John Wesley saw the dawn of spiritual life after having heard a preacher read from Martin Luther's Preface to the Book of Romans. God changed the course of Augustine's life after the Spirit applied the balm of God's Word to his ailing heart.

The Holy Spirit, through *the working out of life's circumstances*, also convicts a person of sin. On his way to Damascus, Paul passed through Galilee. Even as he sought to destroy the Church, the Spirit used the very route of religious zeal to remind Paul of the Nazarene whose followers he pursued.

Another tool of the Spirit to shake an unbeliever out of his spiritual stupor is *the witness of another Christian*. Stephen, "a man full of God's grace and power" (Acts 6:8), had aroused the opposition of members of the "Synagogue of the Freedmen" (v. 9). They fabricated a story of blasphemy, produced so-called witnesses to verify it, and then had him brought before the Sanhedrin to answer their charges. He offered a valiant defense, accusing his accusers of resisting the Holy Spirit and mercilessly murdering the Messiah. Enraged at his accusations, his enemies dragged him outside the city and stoned him to death.

Two revealing sentences point to the beginning of the Spirit's convicting ministry in Paul's life. "Meanwhile, the witnesses laid their clothes at the feet of a young man named Saul" (7:58); "And Saul was there, giving approval to his death" (8:1).

Paul could not have been unaffected as he witnessed "that his face was like the face of an angel" (6:15) and heard him pray this prayer before the last breath of life escaped his broken body—"Lord, do not hold this sin against them" (7:60).

If the Holy Spirit had not been working in Paul's life before, He was certainly at work now.

Resistance

But Paul would still not relent. Even though the Holy Spirit worked diligently to pierce his guarded heart, he kept up his defenses.

In a parallel passage to this, Paul, defending himself before King Agrippa, refers back to his Damascus Road encounter and recites the Spirit's first words to him. "Saul, Saul . . . It is hard for you to kick against the goads" (26:14). In the first century farmers used a pointed stick to guide or drive cattle, especially oxen when plowing.

The goad symbolizes the promptings or urgings of the Spirit. God sought Paul's allegiance. Paul, however, resisted the gentle prodding of the Spirit and refused to acknowledge Christ's Lordship over him. In Stephen's defense before the Sanhedrin he characterized Paul most graphically: "You [stubborn] people, with uncircumcised hearts and ears! You are just like your fathers: You always resist the Holy Spirit!" (7:51).

In Genesis God said, "My Spirit shall not strive with man forever" (6:3, NASB). It is an unwise person who continues to turn God's Spirit away from their heart's door.

How may a person resist the Holy Spirit?

Some do it by simply *busying themselves with other matters.* They constantly distract themselves from deep spiritual issues. Only occasionally—if ever—do they stop long enough to listen to God's voice.

Others try to avoid the penetration of the Spirit into their inner lives by *changing the subject.* When Jesus encountered the woman of Samaria at Jacob's well and accused her of sexual immorality, she quickly tried to divert Jesus' attention away from her sin.

"Our fathers worshipped on this mountain, but you Jews claim that the place where we must worship is in Jerusalem" (John 4:20). Her statement had nothing to do with the prior conversation! But she was trying desperately, and unsuccessfully, to escape the Lord's accusation.

Others resist the Spirit by *lying about the real condition.* When Peter had betrayed Christ, a servant girl came to him and said, "'You also were with Jesus of Galilee...' But he denied it before them all. 'I don't know what you're talking about,' he said" (Matt. 26:69-70). Merely saying things are not the way they are, however, does not change the real condition.

Conquest

But Paul was fighting a losing battle. He could not escape the Spirit's pursuit forever. There was no place to hide from the searching, seeking, saving Spirit.

The Holy Spirit finally conquered Paul's resistance—by love.

If one reads the Acts account apart from other passages in the New Testament, he might wrongly conclude that God overpowered Paul on the Damascus Road, that Paul had no viable choice.

Admittedly, God extended himself to win the love and allegiance of this Tarsian Pharisee. But God never violated Paul's personal freedom. One may blaspheme the Holy Spirit (Mark 3:28-30), insult the Spirit of grace (Heb. 10:29), and "nullify the grace of God" (Gal. 2:21, NASB). In the end, however, a person willfully either accepts or rejects God's gracious offer. Both the choice and the resulting consequences are his alone. If Paul had persisted in resistance, God would not have infringed on his freedom of choice.

Nineteen centuries later God would deal with a hostile Asian in a way similar to His ministry to Paul. While Sundar Singh prayed in his room in the early morning, he, too, saw a light. He testifies:

> Then as I prayed and looked into the light, I saw the form of the Lord Jesus Christ. It had such an appearance of glory and love. If it had been

some Hindu incarnation I would have prostrated myself before it. But it was the Lord Jesus Christ whom I had been insulting a few days before. I felt that a vision like this could not come out of my own imagination. I heard a voice saying in Hindustani, "How long will you persecute me? I have come to save you; you were praying to know the right way. Why do you not take it?" The thought came to me, "Jesus Christ is not dead but living and it must be He Himself." So I fell at His feet and got this wonderful Peace which I could not get anywhere else. This is the joy I was wishing to get. When I got up, the vision had all disappeared, but although the vision disappeared the Peace and Joy have remained with me ever since.[2]

That day on the road to Damascus, Paul of Tarsus fell to his knees to obey the Lord of all. Infinite grace radically transformed this zealous Pharisee and left him ever after a changed man.

5

Paul
Acts 9:10-19

What Happened on the Street Called Straight?

Now the proud, self-sufficient Pharisee, whose eyes had guided him to destroy Christ's Church, was blind. Paul had found with all others who finally commit their allegiance to Christ that "anyone who will not receive the kingdom of God like a little child will never enter it" (Mark 10:15). God struck Paul blind to humble him and cause him to depend on God.

With the light of the Damascus Road came the saving knowledge of Jesus Christ. Afterward Paul would describe the difference Christ brought to his life. "Therefore, if anyone is in Christ, he is a new creation; the old has gone, the new has come!" (2 Cor. 5:17).

But Paul was still blind, because God was not yet finished with him. Christ's "chosen instrument" (Acts 9:15) must enter yet into another crisis of grace and be enabled to most effectively fulfill God's call.

Ananias Employed

God will often use another, sometimes obscure individual to accomplish His purpose for one of His more prominent servants. In this instance, Ananias will be that person.

His name means "God is gracious." Evidently God had been gracious to Ananias, because he is a disciple in Damascus. He stands in violent contrast to another Ananias who might have enjoyed the same beneficence, but, through deceit, traded it for death (Acts 5:1 ff.). Also, since Ananias said he had only heard reports of Paul's malevolent activity, we may assume he was not one of those who fled from Jerusalem. His home was Damascus.

Ananias *heard* the voice of the Lord say, "Go to the house of Judas on Straight Street and ask for a man from Tarsus named Saul, for he is praying. In a vision he had seen a man named Ananias come and place his hands on him to restore his sight" (9:11-12). As every disciple should, Ananias had previously answered quickly and affirmatively, "Yes, Lord" (v. 10), to Christ's initial call.

Oswald Chambers presents a perceptive interpretation of Isaiah's answer to God's call:

> God did not address the call to Isaiah; Isaiah overheard God saying, "Who will go for us?" The call of God is not for the special few, it is for everyone. . . . God did not lay a strong compulsion on Isaiah; Isaiah was in the presence of God and he overheard the call, and realized that there was nothing else for him but to say, in conscious freedom, "Here am I, send me."[1]

If we are living in His presence, we will hear when He calls and answer, "Yes, Lord."

But then Ananias *hesitated* at the voice of the Lord. "'Lord,' Ananias answered, 'I have heard many reports about this man and all the harm he has done to your saints in Jerusalem. And he has come here with authority from the chief priests to arrest all who call on your name'" (Acts 9:13-14). Ananias saw only a man with a bad reputation. God, however, saw what Paul was to become through grace.

When the church in Damascus gathered for prayer, they probably prayed often for God to deliver them from the maniacal malice of Paul. But—like those praying for Peter's deliverance from imprisonment—they prayed with little or no faith. How surprised Ananias must have been when he realized God had answered his prayer!

Ananias' hesitation was not necessarily sinful. Natural human fear and a desire to be sure it was God's voice he had heard probably prompted him to question. If, however, he had persisted, then his hesitation would have become disobedience.

After Ananias had heard, and hesitated, he *heeded* the Lord's voice. "Then Ananias went . . ." (Acts 9:17). When we fully discern the Lord's leading, we must move with dispatch to obey.

Paul resembles a 20th-century disciple who also merited the mistrust of the Christian community. When Charles "Chuck" Colson, infamous Watergate hatchet man, claimed to have accepted Christ, the believers hesitated to accept him.

Sen. Harold Hughes, a well-known Christian on Capitol Hill, was especially skeptical. But Doug Coe set up a meeting between the two in the home of a mutual friend. Well into a strained evening Senator Hughes spoke abruptly: "I hear you have made a commitment to Christ, Chuck. Will you tell us about it?"

So, haltingly Charles Colson recounted the events that led him to accept Christ as his Savior. After a few moments of silence Hughes spoke. "That's all I need to know. Chuck, you have accepted Jesus and He has forgiven you. I do the same. I love you now as my brother in Christ. I will stand with you, defend you anywhere, and trust you with anything I have."[2]

With that the senator rose and embraced the new disciple, welcoming him into the Christian fellowship. So Ananias, "placing his hands on Saul . . . said, 'Brother Saul . . .'" (Acts 9:17).

Paul Empowered

God employed Ananias for the purpose of restoring Paul's sight and conferring upon him the gift of the Holy Spirit. He said, "'Brother Saul, the Lord . . . has sent me so that you may see again and be filled with the Holy Spirit'" (ibid.).

Paul's conversion was a monumental event in the apostle's life, and we ought not to underrate it. But Paul could never have accomplished what he did without the sanctifying fullness of the Spirit, and he had yet to be filled with His presence.

Paul's experience with the Holy Spirit teaches us several important truths about the gift of the Spirit in the Christian life.

First, we learn that *it is possible to be filled with the Holy Spirit*. Throughout the Acts account we read of so many who were filled with or full of the Spirit. Peter (4:8), Stephen (7:55), Philip (6:3, 5), Barnabas (11:24)—all the principals in Acts—were said to be Spirit-filled. Paul prays for the Ephesian Christians, "That you may be filled to the measure of all the fullness of God" (3:19).

But before a vessel can be filled, it must first be emptied. Every unsanctified Christian holds his life tightly in his hand like a sponge. We can only be filled when we release our grip on our self-life and let Him fill us. Not until we surrender can we absorb Him fully. When we let go, however, He fills us like water fills a sponge.

Second, we learn that *cleansing and empowerment accompany the fullness of the Spirit.* No one can perform any kind of effective service for God without a clean heart. Sin short-circuits the connection between us and our divine Source of power. Peter clearly identified cleansing as a primary activity of the Holy Spirit (Acts 15:8-9), and Jesus himself promised power to witness when the Holy Spirit comes to indwell the believer (1:8).

Paul's own life illustrates the necessity of a pure heart and an empowered service. He could never have accomplished the giant tasks God assigned him unless he had been filled with the Holy Spirit.

Third, we learn from Paul's experience that *this infilling is subsequent to conversion.* Very obviously Paul was converted to Christ on the Damascus Road and *later* filled with the Spirit in the house on Straight Street. On the way to Damascus, Paul received all of the Holy Spirit. But not until Ananias laid his hands on him did the Holy Spirit get all of Paul.

Some, however, believe that a person is born of the Spirit and filled with the Spirit at the same time. Donald Metz cites three serious biblical weaknesses in this theory:

> First, the Bible *does* present examples of some people who certainly would be accepted as Christian who had a second crisis. Second, if a person is sanctified (filled with the Spirit) at the time he is regenerated, then all the commands and exhortations to be holy are given to sinners, who are prospects for salvation. . . . Third, the New Testament recognizes that many were Chris-

tians . . . and yet exhorts them to go on to a life of cleansing and of holiness.[3]

Still others teach a progressive theory of sanctification. Since sanctification results from growth, and we are always growing, they say sanctification is never completed. But, while growth both leads up to and away from the baptism with the Holy Spirit, in a definite moment of time the Spirit accomplishes such a work. Just as a person can row in a boat but not row into one, so a Christian grows *in* grace, but does not grow *into* grace.

Then, there are those who believe that no such full cleansing by the Holy Spirit is possible in this life. They reason that sin is inherent in the human body (physical and mental), and, therefore, cannot be cleansed as long as we inhabit this frame. According to this view, the Spirit's cleansing takes place at death.

But all the evidence in Acts and in the rest of the New Testament indicates that conversion and the infilling with the Holy Spirit are two distinct and separate works of God's grace.

Later in Paul's ministry he addressed a group of Christians in Thessalonica and commended them for their "work produced by faith . . . labor prompted by love, and . . . endurance inspired by hope" (1 Thess. 1:3). There can be no doubt these had experienced genuine conversion.

Yet Paul recognized a deficiency in their experience and wrote later in his letter, "Night and day we pray most earnestly that we may see you again and supply *what is lacking in your faith*" (3:10).

Near the end of his communication Paul prays for God to supply their lack. "May God himself, the God of peace, sanctify you (make you holy by the infilling with the Holy Spirit) through and through" (5:23).

Fourth, we learn that *we may be filled with the Spirit instantaneously*. When Ananias laid his hands on Paul,

43

"Immediately, something like scales fell from Saul's eyes, and he could see again" (Acts 9:18). Of course, it was not the laying on of hands that was crucial to Paul's receiving the Holy Spirit, but his surrender and faith.

Paul's experience is no isolated incident; it represents the entire tenor of New Testament teaching. In Christian experience Spirit-fullness follows conversion. All the evidence points to a second definite work of divine grace in the believer's heart, available now, and providing the believer cleansing and empowerment.

So Paul carried Christ's name "before the Gentiles and their kings and before the people of Israel" (Acts 9:15), and did suffer much for His name. But he did not go alone; Christ went with him in the presence and power of His Spirit. And He will do the same for present-day disciples.

6

Cornelius
Acts 10:1-7

The Sermon that Was Interrupted

The name Cornelius, although not very common today, was especially popular in the Roman Empire. In 82 B.C. Publius Cornelius Sulla freed 10,000 slaves and became a national hero. For many years after mothers named their sons Cornelius.

Very appropriately God sent the Holy Spirit to baptize a man named Cornelius. The Holy Spirit does not limit His ministry to the wealthy, the prestigious, or the educated. He is the Spirit of the common man, and He longs to enter the open hearts of all believers who beckon Him. He seeks to cleanse and empower every ordinary Christian and give them extraordinary power for holy living and effective service.

Cornelius' encounter with the Holy Spirit marks a crucial transition in the life of the Early Church. Until now most converts to Christianity had Jewish ties; the gospel had not yet broken out of the old wineskins. But God's plan of redemption was destined to reach around the world, and Cornelius would play a vital role in the unfolding drama.

This passage is often called the Gentile Pentecost. Jesus had given Peter the keys of the Kingdom, and now he would use those keys to unlock the door of personal salvation to all non-Jews.

The Correspondence of the Situations

Several questions arise when we call this event the Gentile Pentecost and identify it with the original Day of Pentecost recorded in Acts 2. Is the Gentile Pentecost similar to the Day of Pentecost? If so, how much is it similar? What do the two have in common? Are they essentially the same? Clues recorded in this passage give us the answers we seek.

Both Peter and his travelling companions believed the Cornelius clan had received the same baptism as those on the Day of Pentecost. Luke writes, "The circumcised believers who had come with Peter were astonished that the gift of the Holy Spirit had been poured out even on the Gentiles" (Acts 10:45). Peter then turned to his companions and said, "They have received the Holy Spirit just as we have" (v. 47).

The presence of the gift of other languages also indicates the essential likeness of these two events. The signs—both on the Day of Pentecost and at the Gentile Pentecost—accompanied the Spirit to confirm to the believers that God sanctioned these events. When they had fulfilled their purpose, the signs dropped off—or should have. The signs accompanied, the Spirit abides. The signs were temporary, the Spirit is timeless. The signs were passing, the Spirit is permanent.

The presence, then, of the Pentecostal sign in Cornelius'

home that day shows the essential likeness of the two events.

Final evidence for the correspondence of the situations comes from Peter's speech at the Jerusalem Council. There Peter reminds the apostles and elders that God gave the Spirit to the Gentiles just as He had given Him to the Jewish Christians. By Gentiles, Peter refers specifically to the household of Cornelius.

Obviously God duplicated the experience of the Jews in Jerusalem for the Gentiles in Caesarea. On both occasions men and women were baptized with the Holy Spirit.

The Character of the Seeker

Cornelius represented the non-Jew. He was a military man, an officer in the Roman army, a centurion. He commanded 600 men in the Italian cohort. Inscriptions found in the area tell us that such a band was stationed in Syria about A.D. 69, and it was called "The Second Italian cohort of Roman citizens."[1] If Cornelius did not command this group, he commanded one like it.

Jesus favorably impressed the centurions who encountered Him during His earthly ministry. When Jesus entered Capernaum, a centurion approached Him and asked Him to heal his ailing servant. Also, the centurion stationed to guard Jesus' cross recognized His integrity and said, "Surely this was a righteous man" (Luke 23:47).

Cornelius was also sympathetic to the faith of the Nazarene. What qualities of character merited Cornelius a personal visitation by God's Holy Spirit?

First, Cornelius was *devoting his life to God.* "He and all his family were devout and God-fearing" (Acts 10:2). He was probably a God-fearer, one who followed the Jewish religion because of its noble monotheism and high ethical standards. He was neither an unenlightened Gentile nor a full-fledged Jew, but he saw the value of worshipping the supreme God and devoted himself to that worship.

Cornelius was also *presenting his offerings to God*. "He gave generously to those in need" (ibid.). Luke uses here the very phrase Jesus used when He spoke in the Sermon on the Mount of giving offerings. The Christian will measure his givng by God's immeasurable gift of His Son.

Unfortunately, materialism has dulled the spiritual sense of too many modern Christians. The cartoonist has Dennis the Menace and his family leaving church on Sunday morning. While his father stands embarrassed before the pastor, Dennis chimes, "Whatcha gonna do with my dad's quarter?" Some Christians have reason to stand ashamed before God because of their meager offerings. When the Spirit came to Cornelius, he was faithfully giving a portion of his income to God.

This faithful centurion was also *offering his prayers to God*. He "prayed to God regularly" (ibid.). Anyone who is praying to the one true God cannot be far from the kingdom. Cornelius may not yet have become a believer, but regularity in prayer would surely lead him to the Savior.

Most importantly, however, Cornelius was *submitting his will to God*. This military commander was well acquainted with submission. As a soldier, obedience to those in command tinted every aspect of his life. He had no problem, therefore, submitting his life to the Lord of lords.

The Chronology of the Spirit

But even though Cornelius displayed these apparently Christian characteristics, he lacked the most important prerequisite for being baptized with the Holy Spirit—Christian conversion. When Peter is recounting the events preceding the Gentile Pentecost, he quotes the angel's statement to

Cornelius, "He [Peter] will bring you a message through which you and all your household *will be saved*" (Acts 11:14).

Although opinion varies on this point, I think that at this time Cornelius had not yet converted to Christianity. But he was moving in the right direction. Cornelius illustrates the "law of light" (1 John 1:9). As a person walks in the light (obeys the truth), God gives him more light. The farther he walks, the more light he receives. Conversely, failure to walk in the light brings spiritual darkness.

Only those who are currently obeying God are candidates for His further dealing in their lives. On another occasion Peter told the Sanhedrin that God gives the Holy Spirit to those who obey him (Acts 5:32). Seeking the baptism with the Spirit is the next natural step in walking in the light.

While not all agree, many relate the baptism with the Holy Spirit to entire sanctification. The *Manual* of the Church of the Nazarene states in Article of Faith X on Entire Sanctification: "It [entire sanctification] is wrought by the baptism with the Holy Spirit, and comprehends in one experience the cleansing of the heart from sin and the abiding indwelling presence of the Holy Spirit, empowering the believer for life and service."

As we relate Cornelius' experience to our own, some very important questions arise. When is a person entirely sanctified? When he is converted or after conversion? Or is sanctification only an ongoing process? If Cornelius was not yet converted, could he be entirely sanctified? And if he was converted, when was he converted?

Here also the opinions vary, even among holiness teachers. But it seems to me that if Cornelius was not yet a believer, his case presents two possibilities: either he was converted and at the same time sanctified; or he was converted first, then sanctified later.

All the other evidence in the New Testament indicates that entire sanctification is a second distinct work of grace subsequent to Christian conversion. But God is not limited in His gracious ability. We can never pour Him into a rigid mold and expect Him to always work in the same way.

The Gentile Pentecost was a special case; God was beginning the Gentile church. It would not be unlikely for Him to use a special procedure to accomplish His purpose. He could, if He chose, easily forgive and sanctify a person at the same time.

But, although God is not limited, we are. The necessity of the second work of grace is not due to God's inability to *perform*, but to our ability to *receive*. He accommodates himself to our limitations. When we first realize our sins, we do not immediately see the further need of cleansing from the sinful nature. We want only to be rid of the awful burden of guilt, and we don't see the need of committing a forgiven life to God for service.

For Cornelius and his household, then, there appears a more likely explanation than that they were simultaneously forgiven and sanctified. I think that while Peter preached, the members of the group believed his last statement, "everyone who believes in him receives forgiveness of sins through his name" (Acts 10:43), and were converted.

If Peter intended to continue and expound the deeper ministry of the Spirit, he never had a chance. Because "while Peter was still speaking these words, the Holy Spirit came on all who heard the message" (Acts 10:44). Since a specific waiting period between conversion and entire sanctification has never been necessary, God then sanctified the members of the Cornelius household.

The path of obedience Cornelius travelled brought him to a crisis encounter with the Holy Spirit. The Spirit waits now to come to every Christian disciple who will follow Him in obedience.

7

Barnabas
Acts 11:19-26

Footprints of the Spirit

The Holy Spirit swept into the first century on dove's wings and anointed 120 of Jesus' disciples. But—except for rare exceptions—clouds of ignorance, sometimes deliberate, have obscured the important doctrine of the Holy Spirit down through the centuries.

Holiness advocates view with some apprehension, some thankfulness, and some hope the renewed emphasis in the religious world today on the doctrine and person of the Holy Spirit. What is not always clear, however, is just what the Spirit is supposed to do in a person's life.

If those who seek Him know when they have found Him, there must be some criteria by which to assess His activity in human life. Otherwise, honest seekers will bog down in a mire of discouragement, even cease their search altogether, and think it impossible to know Him in His fullness.

Does the Holy Spirit make any appreciable difference in our lives? Does His coming only make us *feel* better? Does He make us *do* better? Or does He make any difference at all?

What the Holy Spirit Will Not Do for Us

What, among other things, does the Spirit *not* do for a person? He is not a panacea for all problems. While He is the divine Helper, He does not automatically solve all our difficulties and settle all our questions. What, then, does He not do?

First, the Holy Spirit does not destroy the self. We sometimes hear it said that in order to receive the Holy Spirit, the self must die. This thought needs clarification. My self is all that is me. It is my personality. God created my personality, and the "I-ness" of me cannot be destroyed as long as I live.

When it entered the human arena, sin depraved the self. The Holy Spirit wants only to cleanse that self of its depravity.

Perhaps an analogy will enlighten our understanding. The lenses of many modern cameras show two overlapping circles. To focus the camera, the photographer must bring those two circles together until they blend into one. When the subject appears in the center of the single circle, the camera is focused, and the picture may be taken.

The unsanctified Christian sees two subjects through the spiritual lenses of his life. He needs to bring his affections to focus on one subject—God. Until he does, he divides his allegiance. Jesus spoke of the eye of the body being single (Matt. 6:22).

Everett Lewis Cattell helps us understand the cleansing of the self. When a magnet is passed under a paper with metal filings on top, the filings arrange themselves around the magnet's two poles. Although the magnet cannot be seen, its poles are evident by the two patterns the filings form. Some of the filings attach themselves to each pole, thus forming overlapping circles. Conceivably the filings struggle momentarily before they choose the pole around which they will congregate.[1]

This pictures what James had in mind when he described the "double minded man" who is "unstable in all his ways" (Jas. 1:8, KJV). In the spiritual life, one pole is the self, the other is God. The converted Christian must choose decisively around which pole he will arrange his life: self or God. If he chooses self, he will remain at enmity against God. If he chooses God, this *pattern of selfishness* ceases to exist. The self does not die, only the pattern of selfishness. While we cannot correctly speak of the death *of* self, we can rightly speak of a death *to* self.[2] In psychological terms the personality is integrated, centered around God.

Second, the Holy Spirit will not change a person's basic personality structure. Many sincere seekers of the Holy Spirit have stumbled over the false impression that receiving the Holy Spirit will somehow alter their personality. God made us like we are, and He will never change our personality makeup. While we are often tempted to wish we were like someone else, God wants us to be ourselves.

In a day of mass-production assembly lines, same-looking apartment complexes, and social security number identification, God the Holy Spirit wants to reveal himself uniquely through each of us. He wants to create an original with your life.

Mendell Taylor identifies different personality types among the writers of the New Testament. In describing the sinlessness of Jesus, John the Beloved wrote, "In him is no sin" (1 John 3:5). Paul, the intellectual, said that our Lord "knew no sin" (2 Cor. 5:21, KJV). Peter, however, a man of action, spoke this way of Jesus' sinlessness: "Who did no sin" (1 Pet. 2:22, KJV).

Be content to be yourself and allow the Holy Spirit to mold you the way He chooses.

Third, the Holy Spirit will not make us infallible. We will be disappointed if we expect Him to hone us to perfection in this life. The Holy Spirit cannot and will not sharpen us to a fine point of faultlessness. "We have this treasure in earthen vessels" (2 Cor. 4:7, KJV), and not until we get to heaven will we be able to exchange the earthen vessel variety for the sterling silver genre.

As long as we live, we shall always be subject to mistakes. But they ought never to result from a moral deficiency. The Holy Spirit cleanses our hearts and purifies our motives. Faultlessness? Never. Blamelessness? Yes, by God's enabling grace.

Fourth, the Holy Spirit will not put us beyond the reach of temptation. We must never think that the Spirit-filled person reaches a place where he no longer feels Satan's severe assaults. Paul reminds us that all men face temptation (1 Cor. 10:13). No one is exempt; even Jesus was not. Satan severely tested Jesus in the desert three times before he retreated. And then the deceiver retreated only temporarily. We know he returned because he accosted Jesus again in the Garden of Gethsemane just before the Cross.

While we must always expect temptation to come, we need never expect to yield. Jesus, who knew no sin, enables every Christian to live in the rich realm of victory.

Fifth, the Holy Spirit will not immediately align our emotional responses with our heart motives. A complex society, the infinite variety of life circumstances people face, and the recognition that the carnal nature is only one source of emotional responses all encourage us to tread carefully the path of explanation.

Perhaps in the past holiness preachers went too far in telling us what the Holy Spirit would and would not do for us. Concerning this issue Richard S. Taylor writes:

> We have been afraid to be as specific as our forefathers and tell women that sanctification would enable them to shout when the clothesline broke. Our hesitancy is due not just to the fact that most modern women don't own a clothesline, but to our uneasiness about focusing attention on emotional reactions in everyday situations. We have come to see that emotional reactions have multiple causes and roots, and the carnal mind is only one of them. Possibly the achievement of ideal emotional reactions in all situations is as much a matter of growth in grace—even good health—as it is a matter of heart holiness.[3]

Only constant sensitivity to the Spirit and submission to His discipline will help bring our emotional responses into line with our heart motives. And even then we will spend a lifetime coordinating the two.

These things the Holy Spirit will not do for a person. But we are primarily concerned with what He *will* do for us. If we ever find satisfaction at the end of our search, we must know what we are looking for.

What the Holy Spirit Will Do for Us

The Holy Spirit—walking through Acts—has left His footprints for us to follow. I invite you to follow with me the evident traces of the Spirit's activity in the life of Barnabas.

We catch our first glimpse of this "Son of Encouragement" in Acts 4:36. In order to supply a financial need in the Church, Barnabas sells a piece of property and gives the money to the apostles; they will distribute it according to need. Barnabas appears again in 9:27 as the courageous soul who will recommend a reformed Saul to the skeptical Church.

Luke paints our most complete portrait of Barnabas, however, on the canvas of Acts 11. Some of the disciples who scattered from Jerusalem after the persecution that Stephen precipitated witnessed their way as far as Phoenicia, Antioch, and Cyprus. Most of them testified only to Jews. But a few of the more open-minded went to Antioch and spoke of the resurrection of Jesus Christ to the Greeks there.

Their message fell on receptive ears. Many believed and turned to the Lord. When news of the revival reached Jerusalem, the apostles wisely sent Barnabas—a Cypriot Jew himself—to survey the situation. He encouraged the new believers, brought Paul in to help teach them, and enjoyed a year's ministry among them.

Luke does not tell us when and where Barnabas received the Spirit in His fullness. But there is no reason not to think he was among the original 120 on the Day of Pentecost. Luke does, however, tell us Barnabas was "full of the Holy Spirit" (Acts 11:24). If he was full of the Spirit, then we must assume that at some specific time and place he had to have been filled.

Luke reveals some very clear evidences of the Spirit's activity in Barnabas' life. May we not expect Him to do for us what He did for Barnabas? I think we may.

First, we may expect the Holy Spirit to make us better persons. Luke states simply, "He was a good man" (ibid.). If the Holy Spirit does anything at all for us, He makes us good. No man is righteous apart from the indwelling Holy Spirit. Any other righteousness is self-righteousness, utterly repulsive to God and man alike. These words in a familiar holiness hymn express our sentiment:

> *Not our own righteousness, but Christ within,*
> *Living, and reigning, and saving from sin.*
> —Lelia N. Morris

Second, we may expect the Holy Spirit to make us more humble. In Antioch Barnabas held in his hands the perfect opportunity to fly solo. If he chose, he could be the sole leader of this growing congregation in the third largest city in the Roman world.

The Christians in Antioch, however, needed to become established in their newfound faith, and Paul was the man to teach them. Barnabas set out to find him. He didn't look casually, hoping not to find him at all. The original language indicates that Barnabas sought with difficulty to find the busy apostle.

Paul would eventually overshadow Barnabas. But Barnabas was not so much concerned with his own social prominence as he was with his congregation's spiritual sustenance.

The Holy Spirit will not cohabit in the same heart with stubborn, proud, selfish ambition. In order to receive and keep the Holy Spirit, we must surrender at the point of unholy ambition.

Third, we may expect the Holy Spirit to make us more realistic. Barnabas recognized his limitations. He did all he could and did it well, but he began to see the need for outside help. He therefore asked for Paul's assistance. Had he not admitted his own inadequacy and sought another's aid, Jesus' disciples might not have been called Christians first in Antioch!

God created each of us with certain personal assets, and He wants to help us realize our potential. The Holy Spirit is never pleased with mediocrity. But He knows our limitations and wants to help us recognize them. How much happier and more relaxed we might be if we lived within the limits of our potential.

Fourth, we may expect the Holy Spirit to make us more optimistic. Like Stephen, Barnabas was full of faith (Acts 6:5; 11:24). When Barnabas arrived in Antioch and saw the evidence of God's working, "he . . . encouraged them all to remain true to the Lord with all their hearts" (v. 23).

How much more like Barnabas we all need to be. A little girl who lived with her ungodly grandfather returned home from school one day to find he had placed a sign over her bed. It read, "God is nowhere." Because she was very small and could only read one syllable at a time, she read the sign, "God is now here."

In our sometimes dark world we need the Holy Spirit to give us a divine optimism. God is alive and has placed His mighty hands securely on the controls of the universe. The Holy Spirit will make God real to us and help us to look up. More than a better outlook, we need a better up-look!

Fifth, we may expect the Holy Spirit to make us more joyful. Luke tells us that when Barnabas found the church in Antioch prospering, "he was glad" (Acts 11:23). John T. Seamands writes concerning joy:

> It is quite evident that a great many Christians of our day do not experience "the joy of the Lord." Their lives are more like funeral dirges than symphonies of joy. . . . No wonder Nietzsche, the German philosopher and agnostic, said that Christians would have to look more redeemed before he gave attention to their claims.[4]

Perhaps the reason Christians do not bear the fruit of joy in their lives is because they are not enjoying the fullness of the Spirit. Jesus said, "These things have I spoken unto you, that my joy might remain in you, and that your joy might be full" (John 15:11, KJV). "For the kingdom of God," Paul wrote, "is . . . righteousness, and peace, and joy in the Holy Ghost" (Rom. 14:17, KJV).

Sixth, we can expect the Holy Spirit to make us witnesses. Barnabas and the dispersed disciples had been faithful to Christ's command (Matt. 28:19-20), and He was honoring their obedience as He said He would. "And the hand of the Lord was with them" (Acts 11:21, KJV).

In 1967 Arthur Stace died in Sydney, Australia. He was known throughout the city as Mr. Eternity. He had been an alcoholic, but on August 6, 1930, he stumbled into St. Barnabas Church of England and listened with 300 other men to Archdeacon R. B. S. Hammond bring a gospel message. Afterwards the men were given a cup of tea and a piece of rock cake.

"I went for the rock cake," he said, "but I met the Rock of Ages."

Not long after his conversion he heard an evangelist speak on the subject, "The Echoes of Eternity." That word *eternity* took hold of his soul. He said, "I couldn't get away from it. I felt God calling me to write that word—*eternity*." So—even though he could hardly write his own name—in his spare time 50 times a day for 30 years he wrote in white chalk on the sidewalks of Sydney, "Eternity."

When he died at age 83, his story was carried in newspapers and on television and radio around the world. The Sydney City Council recognized him, and the *Sydney Morning Herald* ran a front-page story entitled, "Mr. Eternity Has Written His Last Word."[5]

Eternity. A timely message for today. The prospect of eternity stimulates every Spirit-filled Christian to hold forth a faithful witness for Christ.

Someone has said that last words are lasting words. The last words to come from the lips of Jesus were these: "You will receive power when the Holy Spirit comes on you; and you will be my witnesses" (Acts 1:8).

We have followed the steps of the Spirit through Acts working in the life of Barnabas. What He did for Barnabas—and much more—He wants to do for every obedient disciple.

8

Apollos
Acts 18:24-28

A Preacher Gets Filled with the Spirit

We know very little about this disciple named Apollos. Luke pulls back the curtain of anonymity only far enough for us to see how the powerful preacher entered into a deeper, more satisfying relationship with God.

Who Was Apollos?

Apollos was a Jew. But he was apparently unfamiliar with the fulfillment of the Old Testament promise of Joel, "And it shall come to pass afterward, that I will pour out my spirit upon all flesh; and your sons and your daughters shall prophesy, your old men shall dream dreams, your young men shall see visions: and also upon the servants and upon the handmaids in those days will I pour out my spirit" (Joel 2:28-29, KJV). Peter said Pentecost fulfilled that very Old Testament promise (Acts 2:16-21).

Apollos called Alexandria, Egypt, home. Alexander the Great founded the city named after him in 332 B.C. William Barclay says 1 million Jews inhabited the city, occupying two of its five wards. The city boasted a monumental library and a large university.

Although obscurity has covered over the origins of Christianity in Alexandria, we do know that Egyptians were present in Jerusalem on the Day of Pentecost (Acts 2:10).

Luke describes Apollos as an eloquent man. The word translated "eloquent" in the KJV can also mean "learned." Apollos was probably both. He might have attended the university at Alexandria and received formal training in public speaking as well as other academic disciplines.

At no time in the history of the church have scholarship and spirituality necessarily contradicted one another. The apostle Paul, the Early Church fathers, and a multitude of spiritual scholars since show clearly the two may prosper together.

But Apollos' greatest asset was his biblical foundation. He was "mighty in the scriptures" (Acts 18:24, KJV). Luke uses the Greek word from which we get *dynamite* to describe Apollos' prowess in preaching. He proclaimed the word with power.

Every serious holiness preacher ought to seek to emulate the example of Apollos. John A. Broadus, professor of New Testament English at Southwestern Baptist Theological Seminary, used his last opportunity in class to lecture on this passage and plead with his students to be "mighty in the scriptures."[1]

What Did Apollos Know?

Luke sums up Apollos' religious experience by saying, "This man was instructed in the way of the Lord . . . knowing only the baptism of John" (Acts 18:25, KJV). The word "only" implies a partial and incomplete experience.

John preached a baptism to signify repentance (Mark 1:4). The medium of this baptism was water. The result was the cleansing of acquired depravity, those sins committed since birth. Jesus endorsed John's baptism by submitting to it himself (v. 9).

Water baptism, however, was not distinctively Christian. The Jews as well as other groups practiced the rite. Another baptism—the baptism with the Holy Spirit—awaited the eloquent preacher from Alexandria.

But while Apollos was not yet *baptized* with the Spirit, he was certainly *born* of the Spirit (John 3:5). We have too often assumed the Spirit absent in the new birth and present only in God's second work of entire sanctification. The Spirit, however, is the Agent in the new birth of every Christian.

For this reason we use the term *initial sanctification.* When the believer is converted, he is initially sanctified; he begins the life of holiness. Paul writes, "If anyone does not have the Spirit of Christ, he does not belong to Christ" (Rom. 8:9). In Paul's classic chapter on justification by faith, he says, "God has poured out his love into our hearts by the Holy Spirit, whom he has given us" (5:5).

Paul also teaches that the believer is to be the temple of the Holy Spirit. "Don't you know that you yourselves are God's temple and that God's Spirit lives in you?" (1 Cor. 3:16).

William M. Greathouse comments on Wesley concerning the Holy Spirit in conversion:

> Wesley hesitated to call the second experience the "receiving of the Holy Ghost." He did not object to others doing so, but he felt the expression was unscriptural for the reason that a repentant believer "receives the Holy Ghost" when he is justified. Apparently

> Wesley was concerned not to minimize the experience of the new birth at the expense of "the second blessing." This caution holiness advocates have not always observed.[2]

Thinking the Spirit inactive in the new birth has also led to a supposed double standard, one for the "merely" converted and another for the fully sanctified. But no such double standard exists. There is only one condition to be born again or sanctified—total surrender to the Lordship of Christ. The only difference is that the believer comes to realize the need of a deeper—not any more complete, but more comprehensive—commitment in the light of the dual nature of sin.

Based on what we know of Apollos' experience, we must rightly assume he knew the reality of Christian conversion. He was initially sanctified. He had set out on what John A. Knight calls "the holiness pilgrimage."

What Did Apollos Need?

Apollos' spiritual journey was interrupted by his journey to Ephesus. One night after Apollos had preached, a couple approached him and invited him to their home, perhaps for a meal. But they had more in mind than just feeding him dinner. They took the opportunity to explain "to him the way of God more adequately" (Acts 18:26).

If we did not take this apparently insignificant verse in the broader context of chapter 19 and the entire Book of Acts, we might pass over or even ignore it completely. Here again, however, we notice another hint of Apollos' incomplete spiritual experience.

What did he lack? What did Aquila and Priscilla share with him that evening around their kitchen table? They must have commended him for his faithful declaration of the Word, but then gone on to explain *full* salvation.

They may have explained to him that Spirit baptism, heart purity, and perfect love all accompany full salvation.

Most Wesleyan theologians agree that a person is sanctified by *the baptism with the Holy Spirit.* But John Wesley never used the term *baptism with the Holy Spirit.* He avoided its use because he feared people would seek some gift or emotion instead of Christ. He feared they would seek *something* rather than *Someone.*

John the Baptist baptized with water and preached repentance. But John predicted One would follow him who would baptize believers with the Holy Spirit and fire (Matt. 3:11-12). By John's baptism God would forgive and cleanse acquired depravity. By Christ's baptism God would cleanse inherited depravity, that inner tendency toward wrongdoing with which every person is born (Ps. 51:5).

The purification of the heart also accompanies full salvation. Perhaps Priscilla and Aquila were familiar with the decision of the first general assembly of the Church in Jerusalem, and they related the proceedings to Apollos.

Certain Judaizers were demanding that non-Jewish converts to Christianity must also be circumcised and adhere to the law of Moses before they could be admitted to the Church. When Paul and Barnabas disagreed with them, the Judaizers thought they should all go to Jerusalem and put the matter squarely before the apostles and elders.

After the assembly had discussed the matter for some time, Peter rose and spoke: "Brothers, you know that some time ago God made a choice among you that the Gentiles might hear from my lips the message of the gospel and believe. God, who knows the heart, showed that he accepted them by giving the Holy Spirit to them, just as he did to us. He made no distinction between us and them, for he purified their hearts by faith" (Acts 15:7-9).

We hear much today about the Holy Spirit. We hear little, however, about the depth cleansing of the carnal nature which the Holy Spirit accomplishes in the human heart. Priscilla and Aquila surely informed Apollos of this aspect of the Spirit's work.

Full salvation also includes *perfect love*. When Christians use "perfect" to qualify their faith, skeptics often take the advantage to dispute both the validity of the term and the integrity of the person.

Most, if not all, of the arguments against Christian perfection stem from a misunderstanding of the phrase. No Christian is *absolutely* perfect, and none ever will be. No human can ever even approximate the perfection of God, or of Adam, or of the angels.

W. T. Purkiser identifies "the man of straw which some opponents of holiness erect and gleefully demolish."[3] They marshall their evidence from Phil. 3:10-15:

> That I may know him, and the power of his resurrection, and the fellowship of his sufferings, being made comformable unto his death; if by any means I might attain unto the resurrection of the dead. Not as though I had already attained, either were already perfect: but I follow after, if that I may apprehend that for which also I am apprehended of Christ Jesus. Brethren, I count not myself to have apprehended: but this one thing I do, forgetting those things which are behind, and reaching forth unto those things which are before, I press toward the mark for the prize of the high calling of God in Christ Jesus. Let us therefore, as many as be perfect, be thus minded: and if in any thing ye be otherwise minded, God shall reveal even this unto you *(KJV)*.

Purkiser comments:

> It is a sad testimony to the biblical illiteracy of our day that any should pick out Paul's phrase, "Not as though I had already attained, either were already perfect," and use it as a scarecrow to drive men away from

Christian perfection. Language can hardly make it more clear that the perfection disclaimed here is the perfection of the resurrection.[4]

In what way, then, is the Christian perfect? He is perfect in love. When Jesus commanded, "Be perfect, therefore, as your heavenly Father is perfect" (Matt. 5:48), He spoke in the context of love (vv. 43-48). Every Christian may not *express* love perfectly, but every Christian may certainly *experience* pure intentions and moral motives. As Dr. Purkiser says, ours is a perfection of grace (Phil. 3:15), not of glory (vv. 12-14).

Many, including Martin Luther in the 1500s and T. W. Manson in our day, believed Apollos to be the author of Hebrews in the New Testament. If he were, it is not strange that he encouraged others to leave "the principles of the doctrine of Christ," and "go on unto perfection" (Heb. 6:1, KJV).

So, in the home of a sanctified lay couple, the mighty preacher, Apollos, was sanctified by the baptism with the Holy Spirit. God cleansed his heart, perfected his love, and empowered his service. As a result of his new and deeper relationship he "was a great help to those who by grace had believed" (Acts 18:27).

A life of Spirit-fullness beckons every believer. No disciple need flounder in a sea of spiritual despair; he may enjoy a more perfect walk with God. The baptism with the Holy Spirit is not an option. Neither is it something only the spiritually elite may enjoy. It is—or ought to be—the normal experience of every born-again Christian.

Reference Notes

Chapter 1:

1. William Barclay, *The Acts of the Apostles*, The Daily Study Bible (Philadelphia: Westminster Press, 1953), p. 42.

2. W. Graham Scroggie, *The Acts of the Apostles*, Study Hour Commentaries (Grand Rapids: Zondervan Publishing House, 1976), p. 49.

3. A. T. Robertson, *Word Pictures in the New Testament* (Nashville: Broadman Press, 1930), 8:59.

4. Dr. George Engel, "Can Your Emotions Kill You?" *Reader's Digest*, April, 1978, p. 133.

5. Ibid.

Chapter 3:

1. Alexander Maclaren, *Expositions of Holy Scripture* (Grand Rapids: Wm. B. Eerdmans Publishing Co., 1959), 8:257.

2. J. Sidlow Baxter, *Does God Still Guide?* (Grand Rapids: Zondervan Publishing House, 1971), pp. 79-80.

Chapter 4:

1. W. T. Purkiser, Richard S. Taylor, and Willard H. Taylor, *God, Man, and Salvation* (Kansas City: Beacon Hill Press of Kansas City, 1977), p. 431.

2. F. F. Bruce, *Commentary on the Book of Acts*, New International Commentary (Grand Rapids: Wm. B. Eerdmans Publishing Co., 1954), pp. 196-97.

Chapter 5:

1. Oswald Chambers, *My Utmost for His Highest* (New York: Dodd, Mead & Co., 1935), p. 14.

2. Charles W. Colson, *Born Again* (Old Tappan, N.J.: Chosen Books, Inc., distributed by Fleming H. Revell Co., 1976), p. 150.

3. Donald S. Metz, *Studies in Biblical Holiness* (Kansas City: Beacon Hill Press of Kansas City, 1971), p. 154.

Chapter 6:

1. Bruce, *Commentary on the Book of Acts*, p. 215.

Chapter 7:

1. Everett Lewis Cattell, *The Spirit of Holiness* (Grand Rapids: William B. Eerdmans Publishing Co., 1963), pp. 25-26.

2. Ibid.

3. Richard S. Taylor, *Preaching Holiness Today* (Kansas City: Beacon Hill Press of Kansas City, 1968), pp. 174-75.

4. John T. Seamands, *On Tiptoe with Joy* (Kansas City: Beacon Hill Press of Kansas City, 1967), p. 10.

5. David Nicholas, "Mr. Eternity," *Decision*, March, 1972, p. 2.

Chapter 8:

1. Robertson, 8:307.

2. Kenneth E. Geiger, comp., *The Word and the Doctrine* (Kansas City: Beacon Hill Press of Kansas City, 1965), p. 217.

3. W. T. Purkiser, *Sanctification and Its Synonyms* (Kansas City: Beacon Hill Press of Kansas City, 1961), p. 68.

4. Ibid., p. 69.